The Proverbs Devotional Challenge

31 Daily Devotions to Deepen Your Knowledge, Wisdom, and Understanding

Alan Vermilye

BROWN CHAIR BOOKS
BOOKS THAT INSPIRE

The Proverbs Devotional Challenge

31 Daily Devotions to Deepen Your Knowledge, Wisdom, and Understanding

Copyright © 2023 Alan Vermilye
Brown Chair Books

ISBN-13 Paperback: 978-1-948481-40-3
ISBN-13 Hardback: 978-1-948481-42-7

To learn more about this book or to order additional copies, visit www.BrownChairBooks.com.

Version 1

Contents

Introduction   V

1. Day 1: Proverbs 1   1

2. Day 2: Proverbs 2   4

3. Day 3: Proverbs 3   7

4. Day 4: Proverbs 4   10

5. Day 5: Proverbs 5   13

6. Day 6: Proverbs 6   16

7. Day 7: Proverbs 7   19

8. Day 8: Proverbs 8   22

9. Day 9: Proverbs 9   25

10. Day 10: Proverbs 10   28

11. Day 11: Proverbs 11   31

12. Day 12: Proverbs 12   34

13. Day 13: Proverbs 13   37

14. Day 14: Proverbs 14   40

15. Day 15: Proverbs 15   43

16. Day 16: Proverbs 16   46

17. Day 17: Proverbs 17   49

18. Day 18: Proverbs 18   52

19. Day 19: Proverbs 19   55

20. Day 20: Proverbs 20   58

21. Day 21: Proverbs 21   61

22. Day 22: Proverbs 22   64

23. Day 23: Proverbs 23   67

24. Day 24: Proverbs 24   70

25. Day 25: Proverbs 25   73

26. Day 26: Proverbs 26   76

27. Day 27: Proverbs 27   79

28. Day 28: Proverbs 28   82

29. Day 29: Proverbs 29   85

30. Day 30: Proverbs 30   88

31. Day 31: Proverbs 31   91

Introduction

I'M DELIGHTED THAT YOU'VE chosen to take on *The Proverbs Devotional Challenge*. The thirty-one days in this book are carefully crafted to help you extrapolate the knowledge, wisdom, and understanding from a book penned by the wisest man to ever live. Although it is a challenge, it's an achievable task for anyone that sets their mind to it. We'll get to more about how the challenge works in just a moment, but first, let's explore the book of Proverbs in greater detail.

Although Solomon is widely credited as the book's author, it also features contributions from Agur, son of Jakek, King Lemuel (or his mother), and a few other wise men who have remained unnamed throughout history. Most proverbs are easy to remember because they're usually short and offer insight into everyday life experiences, although some have more extensive discourse. Sometimes entire proverbs are repeated or slightly varied to make a related or even entirely different point.

Proverbial sayings are not to be interpreted as prophecies, promises, or guarantees. They are prescriptive statements that generally hold true but are not without exception. For example, Proverbs 10:3 suggests that the righteous will never go hungry, while the wicked will go without. As much as we wish it weren't so, sometimes the righteous suffer while the wicked prosper. Yet when looked at as a whole, Scripture tells us that whether or not the righteous and wicked receive their deserved consequences on Earth, there is a certainty of recompense after death. Rather than making promises, proverbs advise us on the best way to achieve a desired outcome, assuming all other factors are equal.

Even though it was written thousands of years ago, Proverbs contains practical wisdom that transcends generations. You would be hard-pressed to find a life situation that isn't covered by at least one of these proverbs. You'll find wisdom on a variety of topics, including family, raising children, the home, work, laziness, leadership, employer–employee relationships, sexual immorality, friendship, money management, obtaining wealth, poverty, trust, wine, sleep, enemies, neighbors, pride, shame, the heart, the mind, sin, wickedness, and much more.

The primary objective of a proverb is to help people make wise decisions that lead to positive outcomes in life. By following its instruction, one can lead a more fulfilling life with healthier relationships, honest business dealings, and a strong moral compass. The practical wisdom contained within the book is grounded in the fear of the Lord from the first page to the last.

To prepare for your challenge, let's go over some instructions:

1. Schedule a thirty-minute window each day for your devotion. This amount of time should be sufficient, but feel free to take more if needed.

2. For thirty-one days straight, read one chapter from Proverbs in your Bible, the corresponding daily reflection in the devotional, and then reflect on the questions that follow.

3. While reading the Scripture text, be sure to take note of any verses from that chapter that catch your attention, evoke an emotional response, have special meaning, or make you think deeper. It could be the same verse I chose or others. There is space provided in this devotional to circle the verse numbers for easy reference.

4. Now go back and examine each selected verse more closely, determining which one you want to concentrate on. Then, write out the entire verse in the space provided.

5. Each day includes a "Journal Reflections" page to capture any insights or emotions that this verse triggers for you. Sometimes one sentence is enough, while other times you may need extra notebook paper to fully express yourself.

Proverbs has thirty-one chapters, which is convenient for reading one chapter per day in a thirty-one-day month. However, starting at the beginning of the month or midway through doesn't matter; the goal is to finish in thirty-one days. But don't let a missed day discourage you. Instead, keep going, and remember that progress is more important than perfection.

I would be delighted to receive your feedback and hear about your progress with the challenge. Please drop me a note at www.BrownChairBooks.com. I eagerly await to hear from you and look forward to discussing your experience with the devotion.

God bless,
Alan

Day 1: Proverbs 1

Read Proverbs 1

The fear of the Lord is the beginning of knowledge; fools despise wisdom and discipline. **Proverbs 1:7 CSB**

WE LIVE IN THE information age, where knowledge is plentiful. With the help of modern technology, we can easily access a vast amount of information and find what we need with just a few clicks. However, having access to information does not equate to knowledge, as the latter necessitates both learning and experience. And according to Solomon, true knowledge begins with a strong sense of reverence and awe of God. This is a frequent theme found in the book of Proverbs as it connects "the fear of the Lord" to gaining wisdom, knowledge, and understanding. The essence of knowledge lies in being able to discern the truth about something and seeing it for what it truly is. When we fear the Lord, we gain a deep understanding of God's character, attributes, and qualities, allowing us to see him as he truly is. But fearing the Lord implies more than just acknowledging the truth about God; it also involves embracing it and living it out. Those who fear the Lord genuinely revere and stand in awe of him and will have a willingness to obey him. It's only through this clarity that we can truly begin to understand the world around us.

Reflection Questions

If you believe that the fear of the Lord is the foundation of knowledge and wisdom, what measures are you taking to gain a better understanding of God? In the past, how have you defined or perceived wisdom?

Circle Any Thought Provoking Verses

1 2 3 4 5 6 7 8 9 10 11 12 13 14 15 16 17 18 19 20 21 22 23 24 25 26 27 28 29 30 31 32 33

Select a Verse(s) to Write Below

Journal Reflections

Day 2: Proverbs 2

Read Proverbs 2

> *If you seek it (wisdom) like silver and search for it like hidden treasure, then you will understand the fear of the Lord and discover the knowledge of God.* **Proverbs 2:4–5 CSB**

NUMEROUS TALES HAVE BEEN penned about treasure maps that bear directions to elusive riches. The thought of these maps alone creates a sense of excitement because of the potential to discover something truly valuable. In this passage, Solomon urges us to seek wisdom as fervently as we would search for valuable objects like silver or a hidden treasure. This is the intensity with which we should approach the quest for wisdom. Thankfully, we are not wandering blindly on our quest. Instead, we have a reliable guide to lead us: the Word of God. It's like a map that shows us the way, and with each verse we read, we feel a sense of purpose and direction, like we are getting closer and closer to uncovering the treasure we seek. However, embarking on a treasure hunt requires more than just a desire for riches; it demands a willingness to brave the elements, endure physical exertion, and confront potential hazards. To think the Christian walk is without toils and snares is a mistake we should never make. But despite the challenges, those that persevere will encounter a treasure trove of godly wisdom just waiting to be discovered, making it all worthwhile.

Reflection Questions

Do you search for wisdom as you would other treasures in life? To concentrate more on your pursuit of godly wisdom, are there any earthly treasures you must forsake?

Circle Any Thought Provoking Verses

1 2 3 4 5 6 7 8 9 10 11 12 13 14 15 16 17 18 19 20 21 22

Select a Verse(s) to Write Below

Journal Reflections

Day 3: Proverbs 3

Read Proverbs 3

> *Trust in the Lord with all your heart and lean not on your own understanding; in all your ways submit to him, and he will make your paths straight.* **Proverbs 3:5–6 NIV**

TRUSTING AND SUBMITTING TO God instead of relying on our own understanding is a constant battle. But let me suggest we do it every day with different authorities in our lives, whether we choose to or not. For example, we might hear a police siren and instinctively pull over, submitting to their authority. When it comes to our health, we trust our doctors' expertise and follow their recommendations without hesitation. Or if a financial consultant warns us of impending ruin, we lean on their knowledge and become more frugal with our spending. These examples might appear obvious and perhaps not fair. But if we're honest, we will admit to giving authority in our lives to other voices as we consume endless streams of information from social media, news sources, and other media outlets. These experiences, both big and small, require us to surrender a part of ourselves to those in positions of authority, whether actual or perceived. The irony is that we hesitate to submit to the authority of the Creator of the universe, who knows all our days. It seems we would fare much better to put our stock in one who not only knows what tomorrow holds but controls it. By trusting and submitting to God, we can experience a sense of peace and assurance that comes from knowing that he is guiding us and making our paths straight.

Reflection Questions

What parts of your life do you find it difficult to relinquish control over and have faith in God's plan? Do you find yourself giving authority to something else without realizing it? If so, in what areas of your life?

Circle Any Thought Provoking Verses

1 2 3 4 5 6 7 8 9 10 11 12 13 14 15 16 17 18 19 20 21 22 23 24 25 26 27 28 29 30 31 32 33 34 35

Select a Verse(s) to Write Below

Journal Reflections

Day 4: Proverbs 4

Read Proverbs 4

The path of the righteous is like the light of dawn, shining brighter and brighter until midday. But the way of the wicked is like the darkest gloom; they don't know what makes them stumble. **Proverbs 4:18–19 CSB**

THE STORY OF THE Pilgrim's Progress is an allegorical narrative of one man's exciting journey toward faith. While traveling to the Celestial City, Christian and his companion, Hopeful, become dissatisfied with the King's highway they are on and select what appears to be an easier path. In no time at all, they find themselves lost and stumbling through a dark storm, unable to find their way back. We must always keep in mind that the journey of the Christian walk is not an easy one. Not every day will be sunny and beautiful; some will be dark and difficult. But never abandon the righteous path, no matter how challenging it may seem. When we intentionally move away from the path of righteousness, we can be assured that darkness will follow. Christian and Hopeful eventually made their way back to the King's highway but not without encountering many challenges along the way. They faced hurt, despair, and depression, and there were moments when they felt like giving up. God's mercy and grace restored them but not without the battle scars of straying from the path. Stay true to the path of righteousness, for even in the darkest moments, God will provide a guiding light to lead you to the Celestial City.

Reflection Questions

Can you recall a time when you abandoned the right path for what seemed like a better one, but it turned out to be a mistake? What was the outcome of that bad choice, and how long did it take for you to recover?

Circle Any Thought Provoking Verses

1 2 3 4 5 6 7 8 9 10 11 12 13 14 15 16 17 18 19 20 21 22 23 24 25 26 27

Select a Verse(s) to Write Below

Journal Reflections

Day 5: Proverbs 5

Read Proverbs 5

Let your fountain be blessed, and take pleasure in the wife of your youth. **Proverbs 5:18 CSB**

I T'S UNDERSTANDABLE TO WONDER if Solomon knew anything about fidelity given his seven hundred wives and three hundred concubines! Regardless of whether or not these marriages were for political reasons, Solomon recognized that if you can't be satisfied with one woman, then one thousand won't bring you satisfaction either. Solomon, with this context in mind, meticulously explains the repercussions of adultery, which range from physical ailments to mental distress, financial instability, and spiritual consequences. Ultimately, you can choose whether to indulge in lustful thoughts about someone other than your spouse, but according to Solomon, God sees all our actions, thereby leaving no room for excuses. So although you may encounter traps and temptations, your actions are still within your control. However, the wise sage understands just how tempting sexual desire can be, so he provides a more satisfactory option: the unmistakable feeling of comfort and security that comes from one man and one woman being committed to each other for life within the confines of marriage. In fact, he identifies this kind of sexual fulfillment as one that is both satisfying and blessed.

Reflection Questions

Have you or someone you know experienced the pain and betrayal that comes with infidelity? What happened because of that breach of trust? Despite the pain of that betrayal, how has God used it to shape your character and draw you closer to him?

Circle Any Thought Provoking Verses

1 2 3 4 5 6 7 8 9 10 11 12 13 14 15 16 17 18 19 20 21 22 23

Select a Verse(s) to Write Below

Journal Reflections

Day 6: Proverbs 6

Read Proverbs 6

> *My son, if you have put up security for your neighbor or entered into an agreement with a stranger, you have been snared by the words of your mouth—trapped by the words from your mouth. Do this, then, my son, and free yourself, for you have put yourself in your neighbor's power: Go, humble yourself, and plead with your neighbor. Don't give sleep to your eyes or slumber to your eyelids. Escape like a gazelle from a hunter, like a bird from a hunter's trap.* **Proverbs 6:1–5 CSB**

ACCORDING TO SOLOMON, IT'S not wise to guarantee financial security for another, as you become liable for their future unpredictable actions. You're essentially shouldering their burden, taking it upon yourself. However, if the loan is not repaid, the lender may resort to seizing your assets, leaving you—at that time—vulnerable to being sold into slavery. Solomon warns us to avoid this at all costs, but if we make a poor decision and become trapped, then we should do everything in our power to deliver ourselves from it. The proverb's wider implication is to avoid assuming responsibility for another person's poor decisions, whether financial, moral, or any other type of decision. The temptation to make better decisions for others as a parent, spouse, or friend can create a false reality that ultimately leads to anger, resentment, and regret. We don't have the power to make decisions for others, only ourselves. To do otherwise is to burden oneself with a debt that is impossible to repay. Only Jesus can carry that burden, and he has provided his blood as security for all sinners. Our debt, which we could never repay, has been fully paid by Jesus, the only one who can save us.

Reflection Questions

Have you ever learned the hard way about promising financial security to others? Does the task of motivating others to make the right decisions leave you feeling drained and anxious?

Circle Any Thought Provoking Verses

1 2 3 4 5 6 7 8 9 10 11 12 13 14 15 16 17 18 19 20 21 22 23 24 25 26 27 28 29 30 31 32 33 34 35

Select a Verse(s) to Write Below

Journal Reflections

Day 7: Proverbs 7

Read Proverbs 7

At the window of my house I looked through my lattice. I saw among the inexperienced, I noticed among the youths, a young man lacking sense. **Proverbs 7:6–7 CSB**

S OLOMON WAS EVIDENTLY A masterful storyteller. While gazing out of his window one day, he explained how he saw an inexperienced young man passing along the street. Calling special attention to his youth, the young man seemingly lacks the knowledge that often comes with age to guide him toward wisdom and better decisions. However, he does possess all the traits common to youth, including desire, vigor, and boldness. This, of course, makes him an easy target for a wayward woman to seduce him with smooth talk, thereby causing him to fall into her snare. Even today, the world encourages youth to live it up now and get their wildness out of their system. When they're older, they'll have plenty of time to settle down and become a proper, religious person. In Solomon's view, this behavior is not only foolish but also dangerous, comparable to an ox being led to its slaughter. God desires to spare both the young and the old from terrible decisions that ultimately lead to the bondage of sin. Psalm 119:9 says, "How can a young man keep his way pure? By keeping your word." Surrendering our hearts' desires to the Lord, whether old or young, is the only way to gain the wisdom necessary to avoid the trappings of life.

Reflection Questions

Looking back on your life, what guidance would you give to your younger self?
What wisdom would your future self impart to your present self?

Circle Any Thought Provoking Verses

1 2 3 4 5 6 7 8 9 10 11 12 13 14 15 16 17 18 19 20 21 22
23 24 25 26 27

Select a Verse(s) to Write Below

Journal Reflections

Day 8: Proverbs 8

Read Proverbs 8

The Lord acquired me (wisdom) at the beginning of his creation, before his works of long ago. I was formed before ancient times, from the beginning, before the earth began. **Proverbs 8:22–23 CSB**

AS YOU'VE SPENT THE past week reading Proverbs, you've likely come to realize that there are two distinct types of wisdom available to us: the divine wisdom imparted by God and the worldly wisdom that comes from our experiences on Earth. Since the beginning of human existence, we have sought either of these wisdoms to unlock the universe's secrets, whether spiritual or practical. Some might think there's no difference between the two, but that's a naïve and foolish belief. On one side, there's wisdom that practices prudence, knowledge, and discretion, while on the other side, there's wisdom that indulges in pride, arrogance, and perverse speech. For those that search diligently, one wisdom outweighs all other treasures, while the other wisdom is freely traded on the open market, making it accessible to anyone. Riches, honor, enduring wealth, and prosperity are all benefits that can come by following one wisdom. The other wisdom leads to nothing but ill-gotten gains, dishonor, and ruin. One wisdom is a creation of God from the beginning of time that is unchanging and true, while the other wisdom is an ongoing creation of man that remains under continuous development. Have you determined yet which wisdom you are following?

Reflection Questions

If you were seeking guidance from godly wisdom for a current decision, what advice would you receive? How would the advice differ if you were seeking guidance from worldly wisdom? Why might it be tempting to choose the advice of worldly wisdom?

Circle Any Thought Provoking Verses

1 2 3 4 5 6 7 8 9 10 11 12 13 14 15 16 17 18 19 20 21 22 23 24 25 26 27 28 29 30 31 32 33 34 35 36

Select a Verse(s) to Write Below

Journal Reflections

Day 9: Proverbs 9

Read Proverbs 9

For by me (wisdom) your days will be many, and years will be added to your life. **Proverbs 9:11 CSB**

T HE SKEPTIC MIGHT SCOFF at such a verse, pointing out that many "godly people" have died young. It's the same argument used by those that claim to know a smoker that lived to ninety-five or an avid jogger that died at forty. There's some truth to what they're saying because exceptions do exist; sometimes the righteous die early and the wicked live longer. However, it's important to keep in mind that these are rare occurrences and certainly not the standard. Generally speaking, following the wisdom found in Scripture will lead to a longer life. The wise have observed and experienced that God's creation follows a particular order, and honoring that order leads to positive outcomes. It's unlikely that anger, jealousy, drunkenness, adultery, gossip, or arrogance will lead to anything positive in the natural order of things. It seems more likely that negative consequences would flow from these actions, affecting your health and leading to sickness, anxiety, hurt, depression, and more. These are all factors that can have a negative impact on your lifespan. By following godly wisdom, you not only increase your chances for a longer and healthier life but also have the opportunity to make a greater impact on God's kingdom.

Reflection Questions

Who are some individuals you know who have lived long, productive lives while serving God with dedication and devotion? What did you admire most about them?

Circle Any Thought Provoking Verses

1 2 3 4 5 6 7 8 9 10 11 12 13 14 15 16 17 18

Select a Verse(s) to Write Below

Journal Reflections

Day 10: Proverbs 10

Read Proverbs 10

Whoever lives honestly will live securely, but whoever lives dishonestly will be found out. **Proverbs 10:9 GWT**

ALEXANDER HAMILTON AND JAMES Madison were persistent in urging George Washington to run for the first presidential election. However, Washington's concern was that his intentions would be misunderstood and he would be seen as simply desiring power. In a letter addressed to Hamilton, he expressed this concern and his wish to preserve his reputation, stating, "I hope I shall possess firmness and virtue enough to maintain what I consider the most enviable of all titles, the character of an honest man." Without honesty and integrity, it's impossible to build a strong and trustworthy character. While Washington was far from perfect, he was a man who could be relied upon to make the right decisions when it truly counted. Solomon emphasizes that to be considered honest, our actions must speak louder than our words. Honesty manifests itself in both the mundane and monumental actions that make up our daily lives. Just as sure as those that live dishonestly will eventually be exposed, so will the one that remains steadfast during difficult times be recognized.

Reflection Questions

Are there any particular situations where you find it hard to be honest? Has there been an instance where your lack of honesty was exposed?

Circle Any Thought Provoking Verses

1 2 3 4 5 6 7 8 9 10 11 12 13 14 15 16 17 18 19 20 21 22
23 24 25 26 27 28 29 30 31 32

Select a Verse(s) to Write Below

Journal Reflections

Day 11: Proverbs 11

Read Proverbs 11

A generous person will prosper; whoever refreshes others will be refreshed. **Proverbs 11:25 NIV**

THERE IS A COMMON trait among generous people. I'm not referring to an abundance of riches or physical possessions. The hallmark of truly generous people is their willingness to make sacrifices for the benefit of others. The false belief that generosity requires abundance can make it difficult for those without much to give. Jesus disagreed with this premise and explained that generosity is not limited by financial status. In Luke 21:1–4, Jesus observed the contrast at the temple between the loud, showy giving of the rich and the quiet, humble giving of a poor widow. "Truly I tell you," Jesus said, "this poor widow has put in more than all of them. For all these people have put in gifts out of their surplus, but she out of her poverty has put in all she had to live on." Generosity is not measured by the size of the gift but by the size of your heart. The poor widow is an excellent illustration of that. We often hold back from being generous because we fear we won't have enough. However, the Bible clearly teaches us that we should not worry about our needs, because God will provide.[1]   Although we don't know what lay ahead for the poor widow, we can be sure that she had everything she needed.

---

1. Matthew 6:25–34

Reflection Questions

Recall a specific instance in which someone's generosity affected you personally. What steps can you take to be more generous and give freely to those in need?

Circle Any Thought Provoking Verses

1 2 3 4 5 6 7 8 9 10 11 12 13 14 15 16 17 18 19 20 21 22 23 24 25 26 27 28 29 30 31

Select a Verse(s) to Write Below

Journal Reflections

Day 12: Proverbs 12

Read Proverbs 12

A fool's way is right in his own eyes, but whoever listens to counsel is wise. **Proverbs 12:15 CSB**

DURING OUR EARLY DAYS of marriage, my wife's family held a large family reunion lasting several days at a state park. In my younger years, I enjoyed exploring trails on my bicycle, so I headed out early one morning, promising to be back in a couple of hours. Without stopping at the ranger station to get a trail map, I set off, thinking I could easily follow the simple dirt trail. As I approached a fork in the path, I began to feel a slight hesitation on the trail that had previously seemed manageable. Both paths had become overgrown and lacked trail markers, so I weighed my options and chose the one that seemed right to me. With every twist and turn along the winding trail, I ventured deeper and deeper into the forest until there was no trail left and I was completely lost. Panic began to grip me as my situation sank in. Looking back, I've found that fools often believe they're on the right path in life, whereas a wise and discerning person knows the value of listening to counsel and doesn't follow their own judgment blindly. Trusting your instincts can often lead to positive outcomes. Pursuing foolish pride seldom leads to anything good. My legs ached as I emerged from the forest six hours later, relieved to find a road that led me back. From that moment on, I promised myself that I would never again hesitate to ask for directions, but I must admit, I haven't always followed through!

Reflection Questions

Can you recall a time when you got lost because you were too stubborn to ask for directions? Are there any other areas of your life where you've been hesitant to seek advice and faced consequences as a result?

Circle Any Thought Provoking Verses

1 2 3 4 5 6 7 8 9 10 11 12 13 14 15 16 17 18 19 20 21 22 23 24 25 26 27 28

Select a Verse(s) to Write Below

Journal Reflections

Day 13: Proverbs 13

Read Proverbs 13

One person pretends to be rich but has nothing; another pretends to be poor but has abundant wealth. **Proverbs 13:7 CSB**

THE MILLIONAIRE NEXT DOOR, a best-selling book by Thomas Stanley, is based on over five hundred face-to-face interviews he conducted with millionaires to gain insight into their journey to wealth. He consistently found that financial independence and freedom are most achievable for those that live below their means, regularly save, and invest wisely. To put it differently, the millionaire next door is typically known for being frugal rather than purchasing items that display wealth. However, this advice appears to have largely been ignored by Americans, which has resulted in credit card debt levels surpassing one trillion dollars for the first time in history. The pretense of wealth seems to have no other purpose than to impress others and maintain a certain standard of living. But pretending to be someone we're not is unwise since eventually the truth will come out as debts begin to accumulate. However, it's important to keep in mind that living modestly doesn't justify withholding resources or being ungenerous. Jesus warned that amassing earthly treasures could lead to spiritual poverty. [1] The fact is, the best way to honor God is by responsibly using the resources he has

---

1. Matthew 6:19–21

provided us. While it's important to save and invest wisely, living modestly allows us more freedom to pursue God's plans for our lives.

Reflection Questions

Do you ever feel pressure to impress others with your possessions to gain their respect or admiration? Have you ever met someone who was incredibly wealthy yet remained humble and unassuming?

Circle Any Thought Provoking Verses

1 2 3 4 5 6 7 8 9 10 11 12 13 14 15 16 17 18 19 20 21 22 23 24 25

Select a Verse(s) to Write Below

Journal Reflections

Day 14: Proverbs 14

———◆◇◆———

Read Proverbs 14

A heart at peace gives life to the body, but envy rots the bones.
Proverbs 14:30 NIV

SOLOMON'S WARNING ABOUT ENVY goes beyond just a simple metaphor and speaks of the very real physical harm it can cause in our lives. According to Merriam-Webster, envy is defined as a feeling of pain or resentment when one becomes aware of another's possession or advantage and desires it for themselves. Solomon compares this desire produced by envy to a cancer that corrodes a person's inner being and decays their bones. Misplaced emotions, like envy, can have a significant impact on health, leading to serious physical consequences. Medical research confirms the truth of this verse. Focusing on what we lack and coveting what others have can lead to a range of physical and emotional stresses, such as hypertension, anxiety, ulcers, weight gain, sleeplessness, and mental and emotional stress. Thankfully, there is a remedy that can eliminate any trace of envy from your system. It's called a peaceful heart. When the heart is at peace, the body can better handle the worries of life and reduce the harmful effects of stress on the body, contributing to better health. Just as a medical examination is crucial for identifying any health issues, self-examination is essential for identifying any signs of envy. We must ruthlessly eliminate envy from our lives by first confessing it to God and then replacing it with gratitude for the many gifts in our lives.

Reflection Questions

Do you ever find yourself feeling envious of others? If so, what do they have that you wish you had? What are some practical steps you can take to eliminate envy from your life?

Circle Any Thought Provoking Verses

1 2 3 4 5 6 7 8 9 10 11 12 13 14 15 16 17 18 19 20 21 22
23 24 25 26 27 28 29 30 31 32 33 34 35

Select a Verse(s) to Write Below

Journal Reflections

Day 15: Proverbs 15

Read Proverbs 15

A gentle answer turns away anger, but a harsh word stirs up wrath.
Proverbs 15:1 NIV

D AVID'S HEART RACES WITH fury. In anger, he commands four hundred of his men to strap on their swords and prepare for battle in retaliation against a wicked man named Nabal. He vows to have killed the man and every male servant belonging to the wealthy landowner by morning. Some may think his anger is justified. While on the run from King Saul, David and his men had also been protecting Nabal's estate and flocks from bandits. In exchange, all he requested was some food for himself and his men. Nabal's harsh and ignorant nature reveals itself when he not only refuses David's request but insults him so severely that David feels compelled to seek revenge. When someone speaks harshly to us, it's hard not to respond with anger. The opposite is also true. If we speak harshly to others, we shouldn't be surprised if they respond with anger. Instead, Scripture recommends responding gently to defuse tense situations. This is exactly what Abigail, Nabal's wife, does as she intervenes and brings David the food he requested before the situation escalates. Her wise and decisive actions save David from falling into the same pattern of personal vengeance and bloodshed that he is experiencing under Saul's reign. In the Gospel of Matthew, Jesus emphasizes that those that make peace will be called God's children.[1] A wise person knows that cultivating patience, kindness, gentleness, and self-control each day is important for easing tense conversations.

Reflection Questions

Reflect on a recent situation where you could have used kind words but instead spoke harshly and caused someone to become angry. If you had the chance to do it over again, how would you approach the situation differently?

Circle Any Thought Provoking Verses

1 2 3 4 5 6 7 8 9 10 11 12 13 14 15 16 17 18 19 20 21 22
23 24 25 26 27 28 29 30 31 32 33

Select a Verse(s) to Write Below

---

1. Matthew 5:9

Journal Reflections

Day 16: Proverbs 16

Read Proverbs 16

Pride comes before destruction, and an arrogant spirit before a fall.
Proverbs 16:18 CSB

WHETHER OR NOT YOU'RE religious, chances are you've heard the saying, "Pride comes before a fall." It's possible that you've even been the intended recipient of this popular adage when someone pointed it out in your own life. The Scripture passage is fairly easy to understand. Thinking too highly of oneself can lead to tripping over one's own feet and looking foolish. In other words, you're not as good as you think you are! The verse is frequently misquoted as it doesn't actually say, "Pride comes before a fall." According to the scripture, destruction is the result of pride. Though it may be a slight variation, it's important to note the difference. The former option suggests the idea of people falling from positions of power. The latter option—destruction—carries a more ominous tone. The Garden of Eden illustrates the most consequential example of pride and the resulting destruction. Adam and Eve's choice to disobey God and follow their own path had catastrophic consequences, far beyond a mere fall from some perceived position of authority they thought they had. We, too, are ultimately blinded by our own selfish pride of our need for God. When one lives independently from God, failure and destruction follow. To combat pride, one must embrace humility and immerse themselves in God's Word. Then our hearts will be more receptive to his Spirit, resulting in a humble heart that is devoted to God.

Reflection Questions

Can you recall a time when your pride led to destruction in your life? What parts of your life do you need to examine more closely for signs of pride?

Circle Any Thought Provoking Verses

1 2 3 4 5 6 7 8 9 10 11 12 13 14 15 16 17 18 19 20 21 22
23 24 25 26 27 28 29 30 31 32 33

Select a Verse(s) to Write Below

Journal Reflections

Day 17: Proverbs 17

Read Proverbs 17

> *Grandchildren are the crown of grandparents, and parents are the glory of their children.* **Proverbs 17:6 GWT**

ON MAY 6, 2023, King Charles III became the United Kingdom's new monarch, wearing the St. Edward's Crown from the royal family's famed crown jewels, a collection renowned for its extravagance. This crown is truly a work of art, with intricate details and 444 precious and semiprecious stones set in twenty-two-carat gold, making it worth an astounding four billion dollars. Solomon's proverbial comparison of grandchildren gathering around grandparents to that of being adorned with a royal crown is appropriate. For many grandparents, the presence of grandchildren is truly a treasure beyond measure that fills their hearts with an indescribable joy. The thought of your life being carried on through future generations can create a feeling of deep pride. I know my three grandsons bring me an immeasurable amount of joy and happiness; they are truly the crown jewels of my life. But I'm also reminded of that Shakespearean expression, "Heavy is the head that wears the crown." The value of the crown is matched only by the weight of the responsibility it brings. Never before have young people been faced with such a staggering amount of struggle and temptation as they are today. It's important for grandparents to be there for their grandkids and not let them battle alone. Be available to them. Provide them with love, support, and encouragement. Above all, remember to pray for them without ceasing. Your crown is a prized possession that should be treasured and protected at all times.

Reflection Questions

Did a grandparent's influence play a significant role in your upbringing? From your point of view, what is the most significant contribution a grandparent can make in the lives of their grandchildren?

Circle Any Thought Provoking Verses

1 2 3 4 5 6 7 8 9 10 11 12 13 14 15 16 17 18 19 20 21 22 23 24 25 26 27 28

Select a Verse(s) to Write Below

Journal Reflections

Day 18: Proverbs 18

Read Proverbs 18

A person's spirit can endure sickness, but who can survive a broken spirit? **Proverbs 18:14 CSB**

CHARLES SPURGEON, FAMOUSLY KNOWN as the "Prince of Preachers," preached to over ten million people during his lifetime, making him the most popular preacher of his day. The author of numerous theology books, he also wrote over 3,500 sermons that are now bound in sixty-three volumes. And despite suffering physical pain for much of his life and having a bedridden wife for decades, he worked tirelessly in ministry, often for eighteen hours a day. All of this had a profound impact on him emotionally and contributed to his ongoing battle with depression. Regarding his depression, Spurgeon once wrote, "It is a real disease, it is not imaginary. Imagination, no doubt, contributes to it, and increases it; but, still, there is a reality about it." In today's Scripture verse, Solomon alludes to the idea that physical illness can often be overcome with the will to live. Depression, on the other hand, can strip away this will, leaving no strength for physical recovery. In the depths of his own depression, Spurgeon found comfort knowing that our heavenly Father allows suffering for believers but that the pain will serve a greater purpose.[1] He later reflected, "...the good I have received from my sorrows and pains and griefs is altogether incalculable."

---

1. 1 Peter 1:6–7

However, Spurgeon had no idea of the magnitude of the greater good that would arise from it. God knew though. For over one hundred fifty years, he has used Spurgeon's writings on depression to provide comfort and guidance to millions of others suffering the same condition.

Reflection Questions

Have you ever been so overwhelmed with depression that you felt like your spirit was broken? Have you ever considered the possibility, like Spurgeon, that your struggles with depression might be an opportunity for God to work through you to help others?

Circle Any Thought Provoking Verses

1 2 3 4 5 6 7 8 9 10 11 12 13 14 15 16 17 18 19 20 21 22 23 24

Select a Verse(s) to Write Below

Journal Reflections

Day 19: Proverbs 19

Read Proverbs 19

Many are the plans in a person's heart, but it is the Lord's purpose that prevails. **Proverbs 19:21 NIV**

A S A HIGHLY DRIVEN individual, I find great pleasure in creating lists. I especially relish the satisfaction of marking off completed tasks as it brings me closer to my ultimate objective: finishing the list! It's okay to set goals and create plans for yourself. In fact, having a goal or plans to work toward can be the driving force that gets people out of bed in the morning and keeps them going throughout the day. People that neglect goalsetting may find themselves lacking motivation and purpose. The question is, how do we know if the plans in our hearts are good or bad? First, a familiarity with Scripture is the key to identifying any sinful desires of our hearts that don't align with its teachings. It's best to immediately reject those plans. Additionally, it's important to realize that some desires in our hearts are divinely inspired and should be pursued immediately in obedience, as God directs. However, what about those plans that are neither inherently good nor bad? We should hold these plans loosely, knowing that they are still subject to God's will and sovereignty. If they don't happen, it's because God has different plans for us—plans that are infinitely greater than our own. The prophet Jeremiah reminds us that God's plans are far superior since they lead to prosperity and a hope for the future.[1] Remembering the promises in Scripture helps us trust in God's plan, which is always greater than our own.

Reflection Questions

Do you prefer to leave room for spontaneity in your plans, or do you like to have everything planned out in advance? Describe a moment when God's plans proved to be greater than your own.

Circle Any Thought Provoking Verses

1 2 3 4 5 6 7 8 9 10 11 12 13 14 15 16 17 18 19 20 21 22 23 24 25 26 27 28 29

Select a Verse(s) to Write Below

---

1. Jeremiah 29:11

Journal Reflections

Day 20: Proverbs 20

Read Proverbs 20

A lazy person does not plow in the fall. He looks for something in the harvest but finds nothing. **Proverbs 20:4 GWT**

ONE OF MY FAVORITE episodes of The Andy Griffith Show is "Opie's Hobo Friend." In this episode, Andy and Opie encounter a friendly wanderer named Mr. Brown, whose unique mannerisms leave a lasting impression on Opie. Andy shows compassion for Mr. Brown by offering him a job trimming the hedges around his house to help him earn some money. As the man is considering cutting the hedge the next morning, he abandons the idea in favor of a peaceful morning spent fishing. His excuse to Opie is "It's the most perfect day to start any job—tomorrow. Most marvelous day that was ever invented. Why, there's absolutely nothing a man can't do...tomorrow." Mr. Brown's excuse aligns perfectly with Solomon's description of a lazy person. It's not a physical disability that's holding a person like this back, just their unwillingness to put in the effort and prepare for future needs. Palestinian farmers plow their fields from mid-October to April when the rainfall softens the ground. Although the conditions are far from ideal because of the cold and wet weather, time is of utmost importance. Failing to plow then means the soil will be too hard to sow in the spring, resulting in no harvest. Those that refuse to plow when the time is right will inevitably face the consequences of their neglect. Benjamin Franklin famously said, "Don't put off until tomorrow what you can do today." We can easily become experts at making excuses and putting things off. To avoid developing this dangerous habit, simply do the work now.

Reflection Questions

What are some tasks you tend to dodge by coming up with excuses? What are the potential long-range implications of being lazy when it comes to relationships, parenting, profession, and faith?

Circle Any Thought Provoking Verses

1 2 3 4 5 6 7 8 9 10 11 12 13 14 15 16 17 18 19 20 21 22 23 24 25 26 27 28 29 30

Select a Verse(s) to Write Below

Journal Reflections

Day 21: Proverbs 21

Read Proverbs 21

> *Better to live on the corner of a roof than to share a house with a nagging wife.* **Proverbs 21:9 CSB**

LET'S FACE IT, SOME of these proverbs are hilarious! But wait—there's more. In only ten more verses, another proverb removes the man from the roof of his house and relocates him to the wilderness. "Better to live in a wilderness than with a nagging and hot-tempered wife".[1] I can't even begin to imagine which one of Solomon's seven hundred wives he meant, but it seems like he created the situation himself! Unlike our roofs, the roofs of Middle Eastern homes were quite different. Their homes had flat, basic roofs that were habitable yet vulnerable to harsh weather conditions and not ideal for permanent, year-round living. The thought of living in a wilderness seems no more desirable. But either appear to be a better option than residing in a home full of conflict. Although we might snicker at the proverb, the key concept presented is a serious one that you might identify with: A household with constant conflict causes misery, whether the wife, husband, or both are to blame. So how do you live with one characterized by a contentious spirit? A good starting point is obviously with a Christian counselor. But Scripture tells us to live in peace with everyone,

---

1. Proverbs 21:19

including our spouse.[2] We should also consider James's wise counsel to be slow with our words and emotions to help avoid conflict.[3] On the other hand, there's a chance that Solomon's advice could have some positive implications if interpreted another way. Perhaps going to your personal "rooftop" space and taking a break from arguing can be beneficial in centering yourself and creating a path for resolution.

Reflection Questions

Can you identify with this proverb, regardless of whether you are a man, a woman, or a child of quarreling parents? How do you manage to keep the peace and avoid conflict in your home?

Circle Any Thought Provoking Verses

1 2 3 4 5 6 7 8 9 10 11 12 13 14 15 16 17 18 19 20 21 22 23 24 25 26 27 28 29 30 31

Select a Verse(s) to Write Below

---

2. Romans 12:18

3. James 1:19–20

Journal Reflections

Day 22: Proverbs 22

——◆○◆——

Read Proverbs 22

Train a child in the way he should go, and even when he is old he will not turn away from it. **Proverbs 22:6 GWT**

Throughout history, Bible scholars have interpreted this child-rearing proverb in a variety of ways. According to some interpretations, the verse implies that children should be raised in a way that nurtures their natural abilities. Rather than imposing a pattern that doesn't suit them, assist them in identifying their God-given abilities, and motivate them in that direction. However, the proverb's more traditional understanding, especially that of Christian parents, is that raising a child with godly principles and showing Christ's love will ensure that they won't abandon those beliefs as adults. And even if that child temporarily strays from faith, they will eventually come back to it in adulthood. This verse is a source of comfort for many parents that pray that their wayward child will one day return to the faith. They wait each day, scanning the horizon, much like the father in the story of the prodigal son, and longing for their child's return. However, confusion arises when we mistake proverbs for promises, leading to disappointment and frustration. Proverbs provide insight into the behaviors that lead to the greatest opportunity for success or failure, depending on the chosen path. Although they provide a fountain of wisdom, it's ultimately the responsibility of every individual to choose their own path and be responsible for their own actions. Studies have shown that instilling religious beliefs in children from a young age provides the best opportunity to help them develop a deeper understanding and appreciation for their faith over time. But there are no guarantees. Ultimately, raising children is a spiritual battle that can only be fought with spiritual weapons.

Reflection Questions

Have you come across any instances of wayward children that found their way back to the faith as they grew older? What advice would you give to a parent that is emotionally drained and dealing with a wayward child?

Circle Any Thought Provoking Verses

1 2 3 4 5 6 7 8 9 10 11 12 13 14 15 16 17 18 19 20 21 22
23 24 25 26 27 28 29

Select a Verse(s) to Write Below

Journal Reflections

Day 23: Proverbs 23

Read Proverbs 23

> *Do not wear yourself out getting rich. Be smart enough to stop. Will you catch only a fleeting glimpse of wealth before it is gone? It makes wings for itself like an eagle flying into the sky.* **Proverbs 23:4–5 GWT**

SOME MIGHT CONSIDER THIS proverb to be in conflict with other proverbs that connect the merits of hard work with the attainment of wealth. Other proverbs admonish the lazy man for his lack of diligence, reminding him that hard work is necessary for success. But upon closer examination, it becomes apparent that Solomon is providing a stopgap for workaholics that burn themselves out trying to earn money only to lose it just as quickly. They're not accused of earning dishonestly; instead, their work has become an idol to them for the sole purpose of making more and more money. What may have started as a harmless drive to work and earn money became all-consuming as their wealth grew, causing them to neglect other areas of their lives, like faith, marriage, family, and health. They burn through their earnings to uphold a certain lifestyle, and whatever isn't spent on indulgences is used to patch up their fractured family or cover health issues that result from unbalanced living. According to Paul, it's not money that's the root of all evil but rather the love of it, as people wander away from the faith in pursuit of it.[1] The desire to become wealthy can negatively affect a person's spiritual, physical, and relational health. Solomon's advice is simple yet valuable: Be smart enough to know when to stop.

Reflection Questions

Have you ever sacrificed your physical, mental, and relational health for the pursuit of financial gain? If you could give your younger self one piece of advice about work and the pursuit of wealth, what would it be and why?

Circle Any Thought Provoking Verses

1 2 3 4 5 6 7 8 9 10 11 12 13 14 15 16 17 18 19 20 21 22 23 24 25 26 27 28 29 30 31 32 33 34 35

Select a Verse(s) to Write Below

---

1. 1 Timothy 6:10

Journal Reflections

Day 24: Proverbs 24

Read Proverbs 24

Rescue those being taken off to death, and save those stumbling to-
ward slaughter. If you say, "But we didn't know about this," won't he
who weighs hearts consider it? Won't he who protects your life know?
Won't he repay a person according to his work? **Proverbs 24:11–12**
CSB

IT WAS A PEACEFUL spring morning in the German countryside as local
townsfolk made their way to the Sunday morning church service. The service
began like all others, with prayer, singing, and preaching, but was soon interrupt-
ed by the familiar sounds of a cattle train passing near the church. But this morning was different as the sounds coming from the cattle cars were cries, moans,
and pleas for help. Everyone rushed to the windows as it soon became apparent
that the cars contained people, Jews to be precise, that were being transported
to their death in Auschwitz. Every week the same dreadful event occurred, and
every week there were fewer people in church. It was then that church leaders
realized they had to do something, so they decided to sing louder to drown out
the cries. The fact that the church members did nothing might sound horrifying
to you. However, they were afraid of being condemned alongside the masses
by a brutal Nazi regime. We find a similar story in the book of Esther, where
the young queen had to make the same decision. However, she made a different
choice, declaring, "I will go to the king, and if I die, I die." Many times we, too,
choose to remain silent instead of speaking with another facing a tough decision,

like a mother contemplating abortion, a teenager grappling with peer pressure, or an adult struggling with poor choices. We're afraid to speak up, maybe even convincing ourselves, thinking, "Who am I to say anything?" Then we turn away and begin to sing a little louder. Perhaps we should stop singing for just a moment and listen to the cries for help then ask God for the courage, like Esther, to take action.

Reflection Questions

Has fear ever kept you from responding to another's cries for help? What holds you back from being proactive like Esther?

Circle Any Thought Provoking Verses

1 2 3 4 5 6 7 8 9 10 11 12 13 14 15 16 17 18 19 20 21 22 23 24 25 26 27 28 29 30 31 32 33 34

Select a Verse(s) to Write Below

Journal Reflections

Day 25: Proverbs 25

Read Proverbs 25

> *If your enemy is hungry, give him food to eat, and if he is thirsty, give him water to drink, for you will heap burning coals on his head, and the Lord will reward you.* **Proverbs 25:21–22 CSB**

T HE URGE FOR REVENGE is a common human instinct that can result in unwise thoughts, words, and actions. James and John reacted in a vengeful way when they believed a Samaritan village had disrespected Jesus by not wanting him to pass through their town.[1] The brothers, aptly referred to as "Sons of Thunder" by Jesus, were not satisfied with just heaping burning coals on their enemy's head. That punishment wasn't severe enough as far as they were concerned. Displaying extreme confidence, they asked their master if they should summon a spectacular rain of fire from heaven to destroy the city. If Elijah could perform such a powerful miracle against the evil prophets of Baal on Mt. Carmel, why couldn't the same be done to the ignorant Samaritan peasants that refused to welcome the Promised One? Jesus was quick to admonish this vengeful attitude, but I've always wondered what was going through his mind. To start with, he probably smirked to himself at the thought of the brothers truly believing they could accomplish this destructive act. But more likely, it disappointed him to see that after all the time spent together, the brothers still believed this was the

---

1. Luke 9:51-56

appropriate reaction. Through his preaching, Jesus had made it abundantly clear that his mission was to save lives, not destroy them.[2] Just as Jesus never forces himself on us, he wouldn't force himself on the people of this Samaritan village either. Sadly, though, they missed a wonderful opportunity for their sick to be healed, their blind to see, and their deaf to hear. But it's really no different today. Every time we refuse to welcome Jesus into our lives, we inflict suffering on ourselves, but not from a vengeful Savior—from a missed opportunity. And every time we attempt to take revenge ourselves rather than letting God handle it, we neglect opportunities to forgive and minister to others.

Reflection Questions

For you, which is stronger, the yearning for revenge or the inclination to forgive? Do you struggle to show kindness and generosity toward those that have caused you pain?

Circle Any Thought Provoking Verses

1 2 3 4 5 6 7 8 9 10 11 12 13 14 15 16 17 18 19 20 21 22 23 24 25 26 27 28

Select a Verse(s) to Write Below

---

2. John 3:17

Journal Reflections

Day 26: Proverbs 26

Read Proverbs 26

A gossip's words are like choice food that goes down to one's innermost being. **Proverbs 26:22 CSB**

B ANANA PUDDING WAS THE dessert of choice for my daughter's wedding dinner. I must confess, I was quite pleased with the decision for two reasons. First, it's my favorite dessert, and second, the caterer was famous for it. I was even more delighted when I found out that there were leftovers for us to take home after the dinner! This, unfortunately, caused an unforeseen problem: I couldn't resist eating it. The more I ate, the more I craved it. I couldn't bring myself to do it, so after nearly a week, I pleaded with my wife to dispose of it since my stomach was beginning to ache. We all have tales of indulging in our favorite food or dessert only to regret it later. When discussing gossip, Solomon employs a similar illustration in this verse. His comparison of gossip to sweet morsels is fitting since both are tempting, are hard to resist, and leave you wanting more. Gossiping may seem harmless in the moment, but it can have long-lasting effects, much like overindulging in dessert. Participating in gossip not only harms the reputation of the person being talked about but also corrupts the listener's judgment about that person—whether the gossip is true or not. By gossiping, we seek to elevate ourselves by tearing down others, with our pride and hate being the driving forces behind it. However, it's important to remember that if someone will gossip with you, be careful because they'll probably gossip about you to someone else. The Apostle Paul proposes an alternative perspective, advising us to steer clear of negative speech and instead speak words that will encourage and lift others up.[1] The same principle applies to both gossip and sweets—the less you consume them, the less desire you will have for them.

Reflection Questions

Do you often find yourself engaging in gossip about other people? In what specific ways can you resist the temptation to engage in gossip about others?

Circle Any Thought Provoking Verses

1 2 3 4 5 6 7 8 9 10 11 12 13 14 15 16 17 18 19 20 21 22 23 24 25 26 27 28

Select a Verse(s) to Write Below

---

1. Ephesians 4:29

Journal Reflections

Day 27: Proverbs 27

Read Proverbs 27

Don't boast about tomorrow, for you don't know what a day might bring. **Proverbs 27:1 CSB**

JUST LIKE THE WEATHER, the future is unpredictable. We can, by analyzing data, models, and trends, predict what's on the horizon and anticipate future weather events to varying degrees of accuracy. Ultimately, though, we are powerless against the forces of nature, like sudden popup storms that can cause much damage. Likewise, the actions we take today are good indicators of what we can expect to encounter tomorrow. But how many times have you been caught off guard by the twists and turns of tomorrow? One moment your life is headed in one direction; the next, it changes course without warning. You think to yourself, If only I had known, I could have prepared myself. But is that statement really true? Given the opportunity, would you want to catch a glimpse of tomorrow? You'll probably conclude that you wouldn't if you thoroughly consider the prospect. Imagine the reckless choices you might make today if you were certain of the good fortune awaiting you tomorrow. Or if you were aware of the impending disasters of tomorrow, what immoral behavior might you indulge in to alter their course? Not only that but the weight of knowing the future would be a heavy burden to bear. That fact is, we don't know what tomorrow brings, and that's something to be grateful for. Perhaps we should stop trying to predict the future and start appreciating the present because it's the day the Lord has made, so let's rejoice and be glad in it.

Reflection Questions

Can you recall a time when a life-altering event caught you off guard, but looking back, you're glad you didn't see it coming? Are you the type of person who lives in the moment or constantly thinks about what's next?

Circle Any Thought Provoking Verses

1 2 3 4 5 6 7 8 9 10 11 12 13 14 15 16 17 18 19 20 21 22 23 24 25 26 27

Select a Verse(s) to Write Below

Journal Reflections

Day 28: Proverbs 28

Read Proverbs 28

The one who conceals his sins will not prosper, but whoever confesses and renounces them will find mercy. **Proverbs 28:13 CSB**

CONCEALING OUR SIN IS an inherent part of being human, almost like a reflex action. Even the most brazen of sinners may hold hidden truths so well that they remain undiscovered to others for their entire life. But it's impossible to hide our sins from God, as he sees everything. The Christian understands this dilemma because they feel the pressure of the Holy Spirit to confess and seek forgiveness. Our actions and attitudes provide a platform for the Holy Spirit to express himself, and when we do what we know is wrong, Paul tells us we grieve the Holy Spirit.[1] The Greek word for "grieve" means to bring about feelings of sadness, pain, discomfort, or unease. It's that feeling of guilt that gnaws at the pit of our stomach, awakening our conscience and sense of morality. Lies, excuses, and secrecy become our tools to hide our sins, and the more we try to cover them up, the more exhausted we become. King David spoke of the heavy burden he bore from keeping his sins hidden, both mentally and physically. "When I kept silent, my bones wasted away through my groaning all day long".[2] Rather than trying to conceal our sins, we should ask forgiveness and let God cover them with

---

1. Ephesians 4:30

2. Psalm 32:3

his grace. Only then will we find mercy and be able to unburden ourselves from the weight of trying to hide our sins.

Reflection Questions

In what ways could concealing sins impact you spiritually, emotionally, and physically? What guidance would you offer to a friend trying to conceal their sins?

Circle Any Thought Provoking Verses

1 2 3 4 5 6 7 8 9 10 11 12 13 14 15 16 17 18 19 20 21 22 23 24 25 26 27 28

Select a Verse(s) to Write Below

Journal Reflections

Day 29: Proverbs 29

Read Proverbs 29

Fear of man will prove to be a snare, but whoever trusts in the Lord is kept safe. **Proverbs 29:25 NIV**

T HE FEAR OF MAN can take many forms, but one of the most widespread in today's culture is the fear of defending what's right based on God's Word. As the world continues to embrace sinful behavior, those that oppose it are finding themselves on the front line of attacks. Despite their sincere intent to share the truth found in Scripture with love, they're being condemned as hateful and bigoted. The impact of these accusations extends beyond strangers to affect relationships with friends, family, and coworkers. And those with any kind of influence are hesitant to engage in controversial topics because they're afraid of being canceled and losing their influence. As a result, many find it easier to play it safe and avoid any confrontation that could have a negative impact on them personally. According to Solomon, this way of thinking can be a trap as silence is often interpreted as agreement. To free ourselves from this trap, Jesus told us to hold on to his teachings and truly grasp the truth that comes with it.[1] If we don't do what's right because of what others may think, we deprive them of the chance to experience the freedom that comes with knowing the truth. Trusting in the Lord does not guarantee a life free of hardship or social rejection. Those that

---

1. John 8:31–32

choose to walk the path Jesus did must be prepared to face the same hardships he faced. But no matter what happens, you'll have peace of mind knowing you trusted in the Lord to do all that he could do through you.

Reflection Questions

Is it challenging for you to defend the truth of God's Word when talking with friends, family, and colleagues? What is the primary source of your anxiety during confrontations, and what steps can you take to reduce it?

Circle Any Thought Provoking Verses

1 2 3 4 5 6 7 8 9 10 11 12 13 14 15 16 17 18 19 20 21 22 23 24 25 26 27

Select a Verse(s) to Write Below

Journal Reflections

Day 30: Proverbs 30

Read Proverbs 30

> *Every word of God is flawless; he is a shield to those who take refuge in him. Do not add to his words, or he will rebuke you and prove you a liar.* **Proverbs 30:5–6 NIV**

IF WE ACCEPT THE Bible as the Word of God, then it's reasonable to assume that he's the one who authored it. And if God is the author and is perfect, how can there be any error in the teachings of Scripture? The logical conclusion is that there cannot be. Although the books were physically written by men, every word was divinely inspired and directed by God through the Holy Spirit's guidance.[1] Paul goes as far as to describe Scripture as being God-breathed, useful for "teaching, rebuking, correcting, and training in righteousness," and necessary for preparing God's servant for every good work.[2] Yet many still believe the Word of God to contain flaws. The dilemma of questioning one aspect of Scripture is that it puts the entire text under scrutiny. How can we have confidence in the truthfulness of any part of Scripture if even one part is in error? We can't. Instead, doubt will creep in, causing us to constantly question whether what we are reading is trustworthy. There are some that consider the Bible to be inspired but not without flaws, as they make their arguments to support their standing.

---

1. 2 Peter 1:20–21

2. 2 Timothy 3:16–17

Still others seek to discredit the Bible in any way possible to justify their stance on a variety of important social issues. Some go further and commit the even more perilous error of supplementing Scripture by presuming how Jesus would react to different cultural concerns if he walked the earth today instead of two thousand years ago. Beware of taking any of these positions, as it may result in being branded a liar by God. God invites us to ask questions and express our concerns, and he hopes we will turn to him for answers to the issues that trouble us. But it's equally important to understand that to believe the Scriptures are anything other than inerrant is to leave your faith on shaky ground.

Reflection Questions

In your opinion, are there any passages in the Scriptures that seem contradictory or contain errors? Have you examined and researched your concerns and asked God to reveal any new insights?

Circle Any Thought Provoking Verses

1 2 3 4 5 6 7 8 9 10 11 12 13 14 15 16 17 18 19 20 21 22
23 24 25 26 27 28 29 30 31 32 33

Select a Verse(s) to Write Below

Journal Reflections

Day 31: Proverbs 31

Read Proverbs 31

Who can find a wife of noble character? She is far more precious than jewels. **Proverbs 31:10 CSB**

As we come to the end of the Proverbs Devotional Challenge, we are presented with an exhaustive list of qualities that define a virtuous woman. Many believe this to be an unrealistic portrayal of the perfect woman, setting impossible standards. But after reflecting on thirty-one days of reading proverbial wisdom, perhaps you've come to the same conclusion that I have. The qualities that define a virtuous wife are simply rephrased versions of previous proverbs. In general, all proverbs contain wise advice on a variety of topics, including the importance of hard work, ethical business practices, money management, caring for those less fortunate, speaking with honor, loving your family, raising children, and more. It seems like the Proverbs 31 woman is the ultimate personification of all these qualities in one wise individual. There's no question that a woman that possesses these qualities would make a great wife, while a man that does so would make an excellent husband. However, it's important to recognize that nobody is infallible and we all make unwise decisions at times. The pursuit of godly wisdom is a lifelong journey that begins with the fear of the Lord as the heart's foundation. The truth is, without the proper heart posture, wisdom will always be out of reach, no matter how hard we try.

Reflection Questions

Who in your life personifies the Proverbs 31 woman with all her admirable traits? How has this challenge influenced your understanding of how to attain wisdom?

Circle Any Thought Provoking Verses

1 2 3 4 5 6 7 8 9 10 11 12 13 14 15 16 17 18 19 20 21 22 23 24 25 26 27 28 29 30 31

Select a Verse(s) to Write Below

Journal Reflections

The Pilgrim's Progress

A Readable Modern-Day Version of John Bunyan's
Pilgrim's Progress

By Alan Vermilye

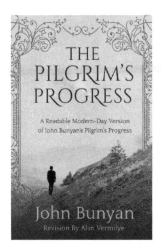

Reading The Pilgrim's Progress by John Bunyan can be a bit challenging even for the best of readers. Not so with this new, easy-to-read version that translates the original archaic language into simple conversational English allowing readers of all ages to easily navigate the most popular Christian allegory of all time.

Without losing any faithfulness to the original text, now you can read Bunyan's timeless classic and reimagine this famous quest that has challenged and encouraged believers for centuries.

What others are saying:

"Phenomenal! Finally able to read The Pilgrims Progress!!!" – Sandra

"What a blessing! Definitely one of the ten books that I have ever read." – TC

"Wow!! This book lights a fire in your heart for sure. Thank you Alan for an accurate revision so that i may understand." – Jesse

"Try reading this book, if you dare. You will find you identify with more than one characters in the book." – Jon

The Pilgrim's Progress Part 2
Christiana's Journey

A Readable Modern-Day Version of John Bunyan's
Pilgrim's Progress Part 2

By Alan Vermilye

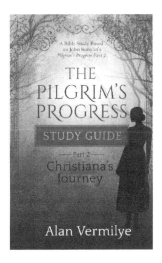

In the Pilgrim's Progress, Part 2, , Christiana must examine her own beliefs while grieving her husband's death. She's torn between following Christian on a hazardous pilgrimage along a narrow way or staying in the place she knows best, the City of Destruction.

The harsh journey is wrought with obstacles, danger, and peril, and many have turned back for fear of their lives. Can she and her four boys really make it there, joining Christian and being rewarded with everlasting life? She just has to believe they can. Thus begins one family's eternal quest to follow their husband and father into the kingdom of glory.

What others are saying:

" have read it several times!! I like even better than the first part!!" – Jeter

"I recommend this book for anyone on their own faith journey, looking for wisdom and truth. It is highly readable and engaging." – January Moon

"Alan has wonderfully incorporated many Biblical scriptures reaffirming faith, life, and love to all who are searching for truth in our world today." – Charles

The Life and Death of Mr. Badman

A Readable Modern-Day Version of John Bunyan's The Life and Death of Mr. Badman

By Alan Vermilye

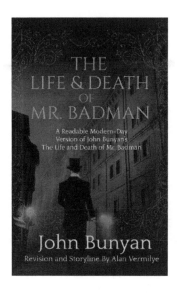

The Life and Death of Mr. Badman by John Bunyan can be a bit challenging, even for the best of readers. Not so with this new, easy-to-read version that translates the original archaic language into simple conversational English, allowing readers of all ages to easily navigate this popular Christian story considered by many to be the third part of The Pilgrim's Progress series.

The Life and Death of Mr. Badman depicts the stages of life—from cradle to grave—of a very wicked man in an evil age and the miserable consequences that undoubtedly follow such wretched living. The book includes the original Bible references and a Bible study guide is available separately for individual and small group use

What others are saying:

"A Very Good Revision Of A Very Badman!!!" – PDT

"This version is much more readable and will no doubt make his story more accessible to modern readers." – MMS

"In a time when many are blind to sin, the book will give an opportunity for them to reflect upon what it means to live a holy, righteous life. Vermilye knocks it out of the park again!" TJ

www.BrownChairBooks.com

The Screwtape Letters Study Guide

A Bible Study on the C.S. Lewis Book The Screwtape Letters

By Alan Vermilye

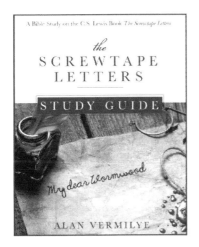

The Screwtape Letters Study Guide takes participants through a study of C.S. Lewis's classic, The Screwtape Letters. This Bible study digs deep into each letter from Screwtape, an undersecretary in the lowerarchy of Hell, to his incompetent nephew Wormwood, a junior devil.

Perfect for small group sessions, this interactive workbook includes daily, individual study with a complete answer guide available online. Designed as a 12-week study, multiple-week format options are also included.

What others are saying:

"This book and study creates a positive reinforcement on fighting that spiritual battle in life. Great read, great study guide!" – Lester

"This study guide was a wonderful way for our group to work through The Screwtape Letters!" – Becky

"Use this study guide for a fresh 'seeing' of The Screwtape Letters!" – William

Mere Christianity Study Guide

A Bible Study on the C.S. Lewis Book Mere Christianity

By Steven Urban

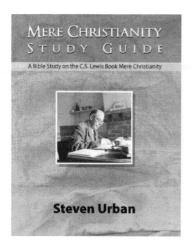

Mere Christianity Study Guide takes participants through a study of C. S. Lewis classic Mere Christianity. Yet despite its recognition as a "classic," there is surprisingly little available today in terms of a serious study course.

This 12-week Bible study digs deep into each chapter and, in turn, into Lewis's thoughts. Perfect for small group sessions, this interactive workbook includes daily, individual study as well as a complete appendix and commentary to supplement and further clarify certain topics. Multiple week format options are also included.

What others are saying:

"This study guide is more than just a guide to C.S Lewis' Mere Christianity; it is a guide to Christianity itself." – Crystal

"Wow! What a lot of insight and food for thought! Perfect supplement to Mere Christianity. I think Mr. Lewis himself would approve." – Laurie

"Our group is in the middle of studying Mere Christianity, and I have found this guide to be invaluable." - Angela

www.BrownChairBooks.com

The Great Divorce Study Guide

A Bible Study on the C.S. Lewis Book The Great Divorce

By Alan Vermilye

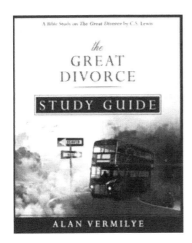

The Great Divorce Study Guide is an eight-week Bible study on the C.S. Lewis classic, The Great Divorce. Perfect for small groups or individual study, each weekly study session applies a biblical framework to the concepts found in each chapter of the book. Although intriguing and entertaining, much of Lewis's writings can be difficult to grasp.

The Great Divorce Study Guide will guide you through each one of Lewis's masterful metaphors to a better understanding of the key concepts of the book, the supporting Bible passages, and the relevance to our world today. Each study question is ideal for group discussion, and answers to each question are available online.

What others are saying:

"To my knowledge, there have not been many study guides for either of these, so to see this new one on The Great Divorce (both electronic and print) is a welcome sight!" – Richard

"I recommend The Great Divorce Study Guide to anyone or any group wishing to delve more deeply into the question, why would anyone choose hell over heaven!" – Ruth

The Problem of Pain Study Guide

A Bible Study on the C.S. Lewis Book The Problem of Pain

By Alan Vermilye

In his book, The Problem of Pain, C.S. Lewis's philosophical approach to why we experience pain can be confusing at times. The Problem of Pain Study Guide breaks down each chapter into easy-to-understand questions and commentary to help you find meaning and hope amid the pain.

The Problem of Pain Study Guide expands upon Lewis's elegant and thoughtful work, where he seeks to understand how a loving, good, and powerful God can possibly coexist with the pain and suffering that is so pervasive in the world and in our lives. As Christ-followers we might expect the world to be just, fair, and less painful, but it is not. This is the problem of pain.

What others are saying:

"Many thanks for lending me a helping hand with one of the greatest thinkers of all time!" – Adrienne

"The questions posed range from very straightforward (to help the reader grasp main concepts) to more probing (to facilitate personal application), while perhaps the greatest benefit they supply is their tie-in of coordinating scriptures that may not always be apparent to the reader." – Sphinn

The Carols of Christmas

Daily Advent Devotions on Classic Christmas Carols
By Alan Vermilye

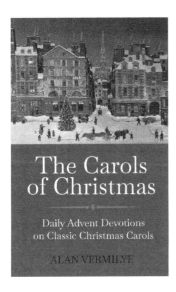

The Carols of Christmas is a heart-warming devotional inspired by some of the most beloved Christmas carols of all time. Inside, you'll enjoy a fresh glimpse of some of the same joyful and nostalgic melodies you sing every year now set to personal reflections in this 28-day devotional journey.

The book is divided into four weeks of daily devotions, perfect for celebrating Advent or Christmas. Each week you begin by reading the history of the carol, followed by six daily devotions that reflect on a verse from the hymn along with a Scripture reflection. Traditionally, Advent begins on the fourth Sunday before Christmas, but the devotions are undated, allowing you to start at any time.

What others are saying:

"Well written, joyful, to the point, informative and inspiring. An annual read for Advent from now on. I loved all of it!!!" – Avid Reader

"This was perfect to read and end on Christmas Day! Everyone should read this one." – Janice

"My wife and I read through this Advent devotional this year and found it both interesting and inspiring. Grab one for next year!" – Randy

www.BrownChairBooks.com

The Carols of Christmas Volume 2

Daily Advent Devotions on Classic Christmas Carols
By Alan Vermilye

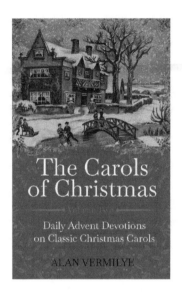

The Carols of Christmas Volume 2 is a collection of devotionals based on beloved carols that will inspire readers to reflect on the true meaning of Christmas. In this 28-day devotional journey, you will experience a fresh take on familiar melodies with personal reflections to guide you.

The carols include "Silent Night", "Joy to the World", "O Come All Ye Faithful", and "The First Noel". You'll also discover intriguing stories and thought-provoking details like who wrote the carol; what was going on in their life that perhaps inspired the hymn; and how has God used this hymn throughout time.

The book is divided into four weeks of daily devotions, perfect for celebrating Advent or Christmas. Each week you begin by reading the history of the carol, followed by six daily devotions that reflect on a verse from the hymn along with a Scripture reflection. Traditionally, Advent begins on the fourth Sunday before Christmas, but the devotions are undated, allowing you to start any time.

www.BrownChairBooks.com

A Christmas Carol Study Guide

Book and Bible Study Based on A Christmas Carol

By Alan Vermilye

A Christmas Carol Book and Bible Study Guide includes the entire book of this Dickens classic as well as Bible study discussion questions for each chapter, Scripture references, and related commentary.

Detailed character sketches and an easy-to-read book summary provide deep insights into each character while examining the book's themes of greed, isolation, guilt, blame, compassion, generosity, transformation, forgiveness, and, finally, redemption. To help with those more difficult discussion questions, a complete answer guide is available for free online.

What others are saying:

"The study is perfect for this time of the year, turning our focus to the reason for the season—Jesus—and the gift of redemption we have through him." – Connie

"I used this for an adult Sunday School class. We all loved it!" – John

"This study is wonderful!" – Lori

"I found this a refreshing look at the Bible through the eyes of Ebenezer Scrooge's life." – Lynelle

It's a Wonderful Life Study Guide

A Bible Study Based on the Christmas Classic It's a Wonderful Life

By Alan Vermilye

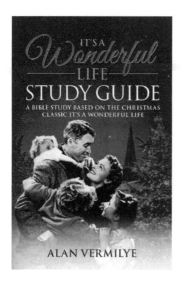

It's a Wonderful Life is one of the most popular and heart-warming films ever made. It's near-universal appeal and association with Christmas has provided a rich story of redemption that has inspired generations for decades.

It's a Wonderful Life Study Guide examines this beloved holiday classic and reminds us how easily we can become distracted from what is truly meaningful in life. This five-week Bible study experience comes complete with discussion questions for each session, Scripture references, detailed character sketches, movie summary, and related commentary. In addition, a complete answer guide and video segments for each session are available for free online.

What others are saying:

"Thank you, Alan, for the unforgettable experience. Your book has prompted me to see and learn much more than merely enjoying the film, It's a Wonderful Life." – Er Jwee

"The questions got us all thinking, and the answers provided were insightful and encouraging. I would definitely encourage Home Groups to study this!" – Jill

"It's a Wonderful Life Study Guide by Alan Vermilye is intelligent, innovative, interesting, involving, insightful, and inspirational." – Paul

The Practice of the Presence of God

A 40-Day Devotion Based on Brother Lawrence's
The Practice of the Presence of God

By Alan Vermilye

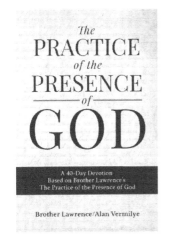

Since it was first published in 1691, The Practice of the Presence of God contains a collection of notes, letters, and interviews given by Brother Lawrence to his friends as a way of helping them turn ordinary daily life events into conversations with God.

Based on this timeless classic, The Practice of the Presence of God: A 40-Day Devotion guides readers on a 40-day journey through the wisdom of Brother Lawrence, related Scripture passages, and devotional thoughts that bring you into a more conversational relationship with God.

What others are saying:

"I love this devotional. It is short and to the point, and thus making it easy to stick to every day!" – Kathleen

"Enlightening new depths in prayer." – Kathy

"This devotional opens the door to Brother Lawrence that brings his letters and conversations to life every day!" – Steve

Made in the USA
Middletown, DE
12 November 2023

42538354R00064